A More Perfect Union (Briefs)

Reimagining the United States as a
European Union-style Federation.

Alexander Moss

A More Perfect Union (Briefs)

Reimagining the United States as a European Union-style Federation.

Alexander Moss

ISBN 979-8-9855678-1-6

Tweet This Book!

Please help Alexander Moss by spreading the word about this book on Twitter!

The suggested hashtag for this book is #ampUnion.

Find out what other people are saying about the book by clicking on this link to search for this hashtag on Twitter:

#ampUnion

For all my fellow Americans.

Contents

Summary

Starting in 2017, mainstream polling firms such as Zogby, Bright Line Watch / YouGov, and the University of Virginia Center for Politics consistently find that support for breaking up the United States into regional sub-groups is growing.

As of 2021, polling across several vendors shows roughly 40% of Biden voters and 50% or more of Trump voters would vote to break the country up - stunning figures.

This book takes a "what if" - breaking up the country into new nations - and develops a roadmap for a constitutional amendment that could make this a reality with the least possible disruption.

The amendment is based on a model in which the current United States is broken into six new nations. Each new nation begins with a copy of the existing Constitution. The new nations would remain coupled in an economic and political union conceptually similar to (but uniquely different from) the Commonwealth or the European Union.

Topics covered include details on the current polling, the mechanics, the economics (including the dollar and Federal Reserve), military, foreign policy, and more.

Structure

To make this topic manageable this book consists of a series of **briefs**, written in plain, direct language. These briefs are intended for general audiences and can be read relatively quickly.

Another title, *A More Perfect Union (Essays)* is intended for those who want to get into the weeds on various topics. For more information on this title, see https://axmoss.com/.

Citations

This book uses common, easily verifiable data and citations whenever possible. In many cases this includes links to sites such as Wikipedia to encourage further reading and research. Other typical sources include the US Census Bureau and the Congressional Budget Office.

While Wikipedia is often avoided in academic material, this book is intended for general audiences. The Wikipedia articles cited include additional links to the primary sources. Readers are encouraged to explore this material in greater detail.

Manuscript Review and Bias

I asked roughly thirty people from across a wide spectrum of American life to review draft manuscripts of this book. Some were friends and family, many were complete strangers hired through various online sites.

For a large number of the people who don't follow politics closely, simply reading the material was difficult. What most of them described was a series of symptoms I associate with prolonged trauma. For the Democrats, the Trump administration was unlike anything they had previously experienced, with the January 6th, 2020 attack on the Capital a major event. For Republicans, the Obama administration, what the majority of Republicans believe was a stolen 2020 election[1] was similarly traumatic. All sides have found the COVID pandemic profoundly exhausting and division.

Many of the reactions from the reviewers were entirely predictable for anyone following American politics. One older man from a very red state agreed with the premise (that the country would be best broken up) but essentially flipped the causation - in his mind, the rise in authoritarianism was entirely the fault of the Democrats, with the Obama administration the inciting genesis. Another older man from the South agreed with the bulk of the material, but disagreed with my characterization of the Civil War as a matter of slavery. Still another claimed that it was impossible for me to characterize myself as a centrist if I didn't acknowledge that

---

[1]https://news.yahoo.com/poll-two-thirds-of-republicans-still-think-the-2020-election-was-rigged-165934695.html

the Democrats were the source of American collapse.

Perhaps the most interesting feedback to me came from a liberal academic in Berkeley, who pointed out that left-leaning individuals concerned about the South seem to ignore the challenges facing populations of color in Oakland and the greater Los Angeles area.

Another individual, an immigrant who teaches political science and fled an authoritarian takeover in his home country felt that I was dramatically understating the risks we face.

It's impossible to write a book advocating any position in the current American political environment without accusations by one side or the other of bias.

I choose to view it as a sort of ink blot test, in which the reaction to this material is most useful as a tool for understanding yourself and your relationship with the federal government. Ironically, the very divisions confirmed by the reviewers served to reinforce the central thesis of the book.

If you believe that the source of challenges in this book are Democrats, you can probably just do a mental find-and-replace while you read and substitute the names Obama, Pelosi, Schumer, and Ocasio-Cortez for Trump as you see fit.

Treat this book as a starting point for an idea. It's an alternative to civil war. It's a bit of science fiction. It's a reasonable modernization of the current federal government into a more democratic institution.

Regardless, I hope you enjoy the material and take it for what it is - a spark of an idea for the future.

Preface

I remember reciting the Pledge of Allegiance first thing every morning in elementary school.

> *"I pledge allegiance to the Flag of the United States of America, and to the Republic for which it stands, one Nation under God, indivisible, with liberty and justice for all."*

Even as a kid I remember thinking the pledge seemed a bit strange. Old-fashioned. One day my public school class discussed the principle of separation of church and state. I was confused - didn't I just pledge allegiance under God?[2]

Of course, the dollar bill in my pocket had an eyeball floating in a pyramid on it. Clearly there was a lot I didn't understand about the adult world.[3]

As I went along through high school and college, I found myself drawn to political science - and not just because it explained the weird eyeball-and-pyramid stuff. Political science is in many ways applied philosophy, and it clarified so much about the world around me. What was going on with the Cold War and the threat of nuclear annihilation?

---

[2]"Under God" was added in 1954 by Congress to "distinguish the United States from the state atheism promoted by Marxist-Leninist countries." Before 1954 there was no mention of God in the pledge. https://en.wikipedia.org/wiki/Pledge_of_Allegiance

[3]It's called the "Eye of Providence," and in 1776 "was a conventional symbol for God's benevolent oversight." https://en.wikipedia.org/wiki/Eye_of_Providence

Why was the economy set up this way? What happened with Vietnam? Why a forty-hour work week, and not thirty or fifty? Everything from the legalistic details to the ways politicians campaign in poetry and govern in prose was (and still is) fascinating.

Most of all, even after everything I have learned about my country, I still find the rhetoric of the founders inspiring.

> *We the People of the United States, in Order to form a more perfect Union, establish Justice, insure domestic Tranquility, provide for the common defence, promote the general Welfare, and secure the Blessings of Liberty to ourselves and our Posterity, do ordain and establish this Constitution for the United States of America.*
>
> **– Preamble to the United States Constitution**

Try reading the opening of the Declaration of Independence with fresh eyes. After all this time, it's still astonishing. Thousands of years of monarchs and emperors and kings, to instead declare that we are *equal*. And that we deserve better.

> *We hold these truths to be self-evident, that all men are created equal, that they are endowed by their Creator with certain unalienable Rights, that among these are Life, Liberty and the pursuit of Happiness.–That to secure these rights, Governments are instituted among Men, deriving their just powers from the consent of the governed, –That whenever any Form of*

> *Government becomes destructive of these ends, it is the Right of the People to alter or to abolish it, and to institute new Government, laying its foundation on such principles and organizing its powers in such form, as to them shall seem most likely to effect their Safety and Happiness.*
>
> **– Opening of the Declaration of Independence**

I majored in political science in college. Unlike many of my peers, I didn't go on to work in the State department. Instead, I moved to Silicon Valley and spent the next two decades in technology. Everything I learned in college - the pragmatic philosophy, the legal concepts, public speaking, the ability to write decent prose quickly - all of it is still useful today.

I consider myself a centrist. I like the idea that liberals suggest new social plans and programs, and that conservatives challenge the economic models underlying the proposals. As long as everyone is engaging in good faith efforts, things will generally work out. While the United States gets a lot wrong, it also gets a lot right as well. For a human endeavor, the country and is an astonishing achievement.

But something changed over the years. A sense that there is something darker developing in the country. In particular, Republicans talked less and less about small government and more and more about apocalypse. The term bad faith came up more and more often[4]. Democrats went from being fellow citizens to the enemy.

Then along came Trump.

I don't view Trump specifically as the problem. I view Trump as the public avatar for something deeper. It's the transformation of the Republican party into an overtly anti-democratic, authoritarian entity. And it's not just Trump specifically - it's the people that voted for him. I believe that they know exactly who and what Trump represents, and that they chose him over the other Republicans in the 2016 primary because that is exactly what they wanted - despite the deep opposition from the traditional Republican leadership.

The idea of a future authoritarian leader taking control of the federal government - one who is smart, motivated, energized and organized - is utterly terrifying.

The twentieth century was marked by authoritarians who murdered by the millions. The takeover of the world's largest military by a fascist leader is a nightmare for the entire world.

I love my family, my friends, my community. I love the rhetoric of being an American - freedom, justice, democracy. I want to live in a society that lives up to those ideals.

I would love for Americans to come together again in an honest celebration of those ideals. But I don't think it's going to happen in my lifetime. The gaps in values and goals are too big. I take those who voted for Trump at their word - they want a different society from the one I want. They have a

---

[4]*Bad faith is a sustained form of deception which consists of entertaining or pretending to entertain one set of feelings while acting as if influenced by another. It is associated with hypocrisy, breach of contract, affectation, and lip service. ... It may involve intentional deceit of others, or self-deception.* – Wikipedia, bad faith

different view of life, liberty and the pursuit of happiness.

I do not want a civil war for myself, my community, or my son.

Perhaps my fears are overwrought. Perhaps things will calm down over the next few years. Perhaps the doom loop of escalating authoritarianism has an exit I cannot see.

But. Just in case. Perhaps another option would be prudent.

The idea for an off-ramp - for this book - first came to me in the early days of COVID. The Trump administration was denying COVID was even an issue, and so states were forming compacts to manage the response.[5]

What if the states… just gave up on the federal government and passed an amendment to make the state level compacts permanent? I'll confess that the idea of a pandemic managed by the governments of California, Oregon, and Washington felt (and still feels) a lot better to me than one managed by the federal government. A watershed moment.

Once I had the basic idea - a simple amendment to break up the country into clumps of states - it just wouldn't go away.

When you are a political science major, you have to get good at writing an essay *fast*. A thousand words is easy, three thousand in a day is no big deal. Every time I read the news, I would pour my stress and thoughts into another essay on the topic.

Just a way to try to get over the stress.

---

[5]AP News, *Governors form compacts to coordinate reopening society*, April 13th, 2020. Also, Wired, *State Alliances Are Leading the US Fight Against COVID-19*

Then, two things happened in 2021. First, a poll came out from YouGov covering the idea of secession along virtually the same state groups I was using in my notes. A mainstream polling firm was now actively tracking sentiment for the idea. YouGov ran it twice, once in January 2021 and again in June 2021... and it showed support was *growing*. For many regions it was over 40%, and in some *over 60%*.[6]

To repeat: 47% of Democrats in California, Oregon and Washington *already* support breaking away, and 66% of Republicans in the South. That's... incredible.

Second, I started sharing my ideas with friends. It was (and still is) a bit nerve-wracking. "Hey, I'm thinking about how to break up the United States into six nations" seemed like a pretty fringe thing to talk about.

To my surprise, I found that people were interested in the idea, but they had a *lot* of questions. How would it work? What about the South? Could it really happen? What about the military and the nuclear weapons?

A surprising number said they had already been thinking about it. I suppose given the polling data I shouldn't have been surprised, but still.

Those two things - the polling and the conversations - made me decide to pull all my notes and essays into this book.

For the sake of everyone - not just in the United States, but the entire world - I hope we can figure this out.

My hope is that by having the conversation, it will change how we all look at our country. Perhaps the discussion will

---

[6]http://brightlinewatch.org/still-miles-apart-americans-and-the-state-of-u-s-democracy-half-a-year-into-the-biden-presidency/

inspire us to come together, to fix the existing system, and reinvigorate the federal government for future generations.

But, just in case we can't come together, it's probably a good idea to have an escape hatch.

P.S. To my elementary school teacher: I'm sorry about considering the "indivisible" part to be potentially negotiable. I still love my fellow Americans, and I hope we can all work things out.

1. Problem Statement

Before proposing a solution, it's important to clearly state the problem.

The focus for this book is the federal government as an institution and the Constitution as the operating agreement for the nation.

Issues at the state, county, and municipal level are specifically excluded from the problem statement. The changes proposed later in this book are specifically designed to minimize impacts on these institutions - at least until the new nations begin passing new amendments and legislation.

This book is focused on democracy as the only legitimate source of governmental authority. The foundation of democracy is the idea that people who vote are clearly expressing their intentions and desires. If someone votes for Trump, Clinton, or Biden, you must take them at their word that they are of sound mind and are expressing themselves democratically. Anything else is doubting democracy as a system.[1]

Failed Governing Systems

Unfortunately, regardless of your opinions, the current system simply does not allow for democratically expressed positions

---

[1] If you find this a challenging concept, check out the essay *Who is Running The Show*.

to be turned into action. Consider the process involved for a party to pass any Federal legislation:

1. Win the House

This includes getting around voter suppression and gerrymandering.

2. Win the Senate

This includes getting at least 60 votes in order to break a filibuster.

3. Win the Presidency

The President can veto any bill and send it back to the House and Senate, requiring both houses to pass the bill with a two-thirds majority.

As a workaround, the President can issue executive orders, subject to court review.

4. Survive Court Challenges

The Supreme Court can choose to strike down or redefine legislation at it sees fit. The only way to remove a Supreme Court justice is via impeachment (which requires 50% of the House and two-thirds of the Senate). Adding judges (packing) or changing the composition of the court requires legislation as described above.

5. Survive Implementation & Regulatory Capture

Once the program is in place, it needs to be funded and reasonably well run. This can be subverted by the executive branch at any time - for example, by defunding. Or it can be subject to regulatory capture - for example, by appointing friendly former industry management to the organization ostensibly responsible for oversight of that same industry.

The bar for passing and successfully implementing legislation has become ludicrously high. This incredibly high bar for passing legislation forces the president to take more and more sweeping executive actions in order to be responsive to the voters. This in turn puts more and more pressure on the Court as a backstop for executive action. This creates a more and more intense set of reinforcing feedback loops.

This loop is extraordinarily bad for democracy. Pressure to respond to a President's base combined with congressional dysfunction forces more executive orders, which puts more pressure on the Court as a backstop, leading to less a less democratic outcome. Everyone becomes increasingly frustrated, demoralized, and pessimistic about the entire endeavor.

It is the position of this author that legislative reform is highly unlikely. It is not realistic to expect significant reforms under the current system. The bar for legislation is simply too high.[2]

If a democracy is not responsive to the needs of the citizens, what is it?[3]

---

[2]As a reminder, while the Founders did intend for legislation to be difficult, most of these issues confronting democracy today simply were not conceived of back then - including but not limited to gerrymandering and the filibuster. The Founders considered political parties anathema.

[3]If you are curious, the Economist prepares a Democracy Index to review the state of democracy in 167 countries. In 2016 the United States fell from a "full democracy" to a "flawed democracy."

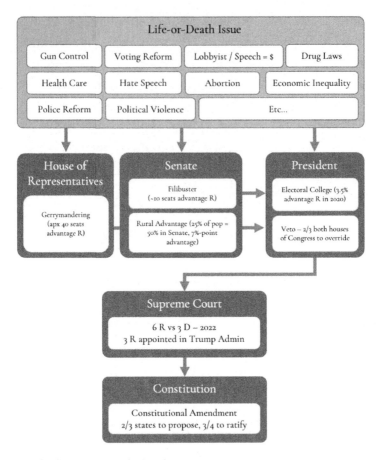

https://www.supremecourt.gov/about/biographies.aspx
https://www.americanprogress.org/issues/democracy/news/2019/10/01/475166/impact-partisan-gerrymandering/
https://pollsandtrends.com/how-rural-states-are-over-represented-in-the-u-s-senate-and-presidential-elections/
https://fivethirtyeight.com/features/advantage-gop/

Root Cause Analysis

Rise of Authoritarianism

The other half of the problem statement is the rise of authoritarianism, specifically in the United States by the takeover of the Republican party by Donald Trump.

This could be a very long section of this book, but most readers already have a well-developed opinion on the authoritarian nature of Trumpism. This book is not intended to change your mind about Trumpism - but it is intended to offer a solution for both supporters and opponents.

In a worst-case scenario, the control of the United States Federal Government - including the world's most powerful, nuclear armed military - falls to an intelligent, energized, charismatic authoritarian leader, ushering in a generation or more of darkness across the world.

If you haven't found the last few years of American politics to be traumatic enough, you can find more stuff of nightmares in the essay *Worst Case Scenarios*[4].

Interest In Secession Is Rising

The Wikipedia article, Secession in the United States[5] has many interesting articles on the history of secession movements. The excellent *Break It Up: Secession, Division, and the Secret History of America's Imperfect Union*[6] by Richard Kreitner provides a highly readable overview of historic secession movements.

In the modern era, John Zogby Strategies articles include coverage in 2017 with *New Poll On Americans' Support*

[4]https://axmoss.com/essays/
[5]https://en.wikipedia.org/wiki/Secession_in_the_United_States
[6]https://amzn.to/39cOo6L

Secession, 2017[7] and in 2018, *Secessionist Sentiment Remains a Plurality Among Likely Voters, 2018*[8]. In September 2021, University of Virginia Center for Politics polling[9] found "roughly 4 in 10 (41%) of Biden and half (52%) of Trump voters at least somewhat agree that it's time to split the country."

Bright Line Watch, working with YouGov, conducted polls in January[10] and June[11] of 2021 and found support continuing to rise over that period.

---

[7]https://johnzogbystrategies.com/new-poll-on-americans-support-for-secession-webinar-on-tribal-analytics-and-trump-report-card/

[8]https://johnzogbystrategies.com/secessionist-sentiment-remains-a-plurality-among-likely-voters/

[9]https://centerforpolitics.org/crystalball/articles/new-initiative-explores-deep-persistent-divides-between-biden-and-trump-voters/

[10]http://brightlinewatch.org/american-democracy-at-the-start-of-the-biden-presidency/

[11]http://brightlinewatch.org/still-miles-apart-americans-and-the-state-of-u-s-democracy-half-a-year-into-the-biden-presidency/

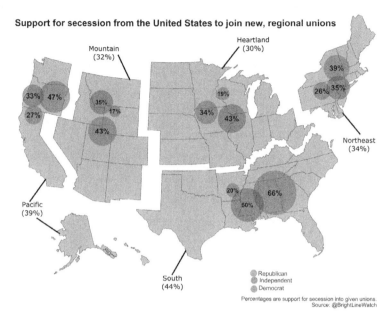

YouGov June 2021 Secession Support

If you belong the majority party in a region, you are **more** likely to support secession. Republicans in the South and Democrats on the West Coast and Northeast are significantly more likely to support secession.

Virtually every secession movement today focuses on a specific region – the Pacific Coast, the South, Texas – and fails to consider any larger picture. By providing a model for all regions to break apart cleanly and coherently, it makes the entire process much more likely to be handled in an organized, peaceful manner.

In brief, democracy is in deep trouble and authoritarianism is on the rise. People are *already* looking at secession as a solution.

Not A Miracle Solution

A common rhetorical device to oppose a new idea or plan is sometimes referred to a "opposition to an insufficient miracle." In other words, if an idea does not solve *all* problems it is deemed insufficient.

The problem statement for the ideas in this book is explicitly *not* to solve all problems. It will not (in and of itself) solve climate change, or authoritarianism, or racism. At the most basic levels, the goals are to increase and invigorate democracy, reenergize the dreams of American citizens, eliminate the rising tensions and risk of civil war, and prevent the apparatus of the world's largest nuclear military from falling into fascism and plunging the world into darkness for at least a generation.

This book is, with all apologies, already ambitious enough.

2. How Did We Get Here?

A brief, non-exhaustive catalog of some candidates for discussion:

1. We got big.
2. We have no national unity project.
3. Our cultural fault lines are viewed as non-negotiable matters of life and death.
4. Our political parties have degenerated into a mess of federalism and anti-federalism.
5. We have a very, very old Constitution.

We Got Big

In roughly one hundred years (1920 to 2020) the United States grew from a population of one hundred million to over three hundred million.

It's an incredible success story. It's also easy to understand that governance of a large population is presents many challenges. The Roman Empire broke apart at roughly one hundred million. Only China and India today have larger populations, and many of the other countries larger than one hundred million face dramatic challenges - Pakistan, Russia, Mexico and others. When does the size of the country interact with cultural drift in such as a way as to cause more problems than it solves?

This question of size is considered in more detail in the essay *One Hundred Million*[1].

No National Unity Project

Traditional American history is often broken up into chapters reflecting the major themes of the period. For example, typical chapters might include:

- Development of the Colonies
- (Civil) War for Independence
- Manifest Destiny
- Civil War
- Reconstruction
- World War I
- Roaring Twenties
- Great Depression
- World War II
- Cold War

Regardless of how one views these events, they all eventually coalesced into a consensus view of how things were organized at the time. For example, regardless of how one felt about the Great Depression and the New Deal, there was clear agreement that the Great Depression itself represented a problem that needed some kind of solution. The question was not "if" something should be done, but rather "what." The goals were clear, even if the means were not.

---

[1]https://axmoss.com/essays/

In contrast with the 1930s and 1940s, the stated goals expressed by Democrat and Republican federal politicians today are mutually incompatible expressions of intent. Sadly, a future historian would likely point to a primary motivation for political action today as *fear and loathing of other Americans*. This is likely a side-effect of the other causes, but it illustrates the depth of the problem.

A key reason "why now" is the exit of the last generation to experience a genuine national unity project (World War 2) has now exited the political stage. Widespread disagreement over endeavors such as Vietnam, the war on drugs, the war on terror and the various Middle East forever-wars tear the nation apart.[2]

This question of potential unity projects is addressed in more detail in the essay *Considering National Unity Projects*[3] - including the challenges facing large scale projects such as The Green New Deal, infrastructure, and a national health care system.

Life and Death Cultural Divisions

Some issues, especially economic, lend themselves to negotiation. For example, tax rates and many forms of stimulus are inherently amenable to simple compromises.

The most divisive issues of our day, however, do not lend

---

[2]For more on the notion of generations as a political force, see *Generations* by Neil Howe and William Strauss (1992). It's the book that really imprinted the notion of generational theory on American culture - every time you use a term like "Boomer" or "Generation X" you are building on the ideas in *Generations*.

[3]https://axmoss.com/essays/

themselves to negotiation. They are generally winner-take-all, life or death issues. It's why for so many compromise is untenable - how can you trust a political party willing to trade away a matters of life and death for a new highway?

Here is a very brief list of typical issues confronting America and the life-or-death framing applied by each side:

1. *Race relations* - murder by police vs. thin blue line
2. *Abortion* - murder babies vs. right to control your body
3. *Endless Wars* - murder innocent civilians vs. killing terrorists
4. *Health Care* - death and bankruptcy vs. government control/nationalization of health care
5. *Economic Inequality* - death, poverty, despair and bankruptcy vs. economic freedom
6. *COVID* - Death or permanent disability by COVID vs death or disability by "unproven" or dangerous vaccines

If death is on the line, diplomacy and negotiation are insufficient. If you genuinely believe your life is threatened, patience is not a virtue. If sufficiently frightened, no wonder some would turn to authoritarianism.

The ability to compromise over real and perceived life and death issues is hugely impacted by generational experience. If you watched friends and family die in a civil or world war, you are likely to be more inclined to try to seek non-military options for managing conflict. If, on the other hand, you have seen multi-generational trauma with no viable options for relief, you are likely to increasingly view the debate with less willingness to wait and see.

The very security brought about by being a geographically isolated world superpower exacerbates the issues. If the country is unified by the fear of nuclear war with the Soviet Union, it indirectly increases the pressure to compromise on domestic issues. No one in the United States has been remotely concerned about an invasion or existential threat since (realistically) the end of the cold war in 1991, and so one of the most basic sources of unity (mutual defense) has been turned upside down.

We Have an Old Constitution

After the ill-fated Articles of Confederation, the Constitution was developed as a solution for thirteen essentially agrarian states. The thoughts and rationale for the Constitution are documented in the highly enjoyable Federalist Papers[4].

The Constitution was very clearly intended to be a living document by the authors, which is why the amendment process was included. Unfortunately, many of the most pressing cultural issues of the day, ranging from gun control to gender issues to abortion are essentially impossible to address with the amendment system.

Imagine, if you will, trying to pass Constitutional amendments to resolve issues such as gun control, voting rights, abortion rights, or healthcare. It's impossible, because you would need *three quarters* of the states to agree. Simply put, these issues will *never* be resolved via Constitutional amendment. Which means that the greatest issues of our day

---

[4]https://guides.loc.gov/federalist-papers/full-text

- the ones that are increasingly regarded as life-or-death –
simply *cannot* be resolved peacefully and legally. No wonder
there is so much frustration and fear.

This implications of an old Constitution are addressed in
more detail in the essay *We Have An Old Constitution*[5].

Federalist and Anti-Federalist

> *"In this present crisis, government is not the solution to our
> problem; government is the problem."*
>
> • Ronald Reagan, Inaugural Address, 1981

At some point in the post-World War 2 era, the Republican Party shifted from an intellectual model rooted in
limited government to a party unified only by a general anti-
government sentiment[6]. It's a very important, critical shift,
one which is best exemplified most recently by the transition
of Republican leadership from figures such as Paul Ryan and
John Boehner to Donald Trump.[7]

There is widespread agreement that one of the underlying
drivers for Trumpism is a broad interest in what is most

----

[5]https://axmoss.com/essays/
[6]https://www.presidency.ucsb.edu/documents/inaugural-address-11
[7]For more on this topic, I highly recommend the book *American Carnage: On the
Front Lines of the Republican Civil War and the Rise of President Trump* by Tim Alberta

appropriately described as authoritarianism.[8] Simply put, authoritarianism is not compatible with democracy. Authoritarianism is the driver behind such strategies as:

- Eliminating the Republican primaries
- Voter suppression
- Allegations of stolen elections
- Loyalty tests and "kissing the ring" for Republican candidates

It's impossible to sustain a democracy in the long term with one of the two major parties dedicated to authoritarianism. Unfortunately, if you are fundamentally opposed to federalism because of life-and-death concerns, the authoritarians are the only game in town that has demonstrated the ability to win elections. The authoritarians only need to win *once* - and then the darkness falls.

We have very real, very serious problems that are not amenable to negotiation, with a system that is incapable of adapting or resolving those problems.

Now what?

---

[8]Must read: *The Authoritarians* by Bob Altemeyer. It addresses the question "why would anyone follow an authoritarian leader" in detail. In particular I recommend the audiobook version for the highly engaging and humorous delivery of such a fundamentally depressing topic.

3. Worst Case Scenarios

For many, horrific scenarios are already here. The United States currently faces staggering concerns unheard of in our peacetime history:

- Massive growth in economic inequality
- The world's largest per-capita prison population
- The most expensive and least effective health care system in the developed world
- Historic levels of national debt
- Staggering death and long-term health issues due to COVID
- Rapidly increasing climate change crises, including hurricanes, drought, flooding, and wildfires
- Rise of overtly authoritarian politicians

Unfortunately, this is the world of today. Sadly, we must consider even more potentially catastrophic outcomes in the near future.

Unmanaged Collapse

In this scenario, it's hard to point to a single incident. Was it the armed insurrectionists that seized the Congress in a bloody weeklong standoff? When a Democrat/Republican president issues executive orders so abhorrent to Red or Blue states the governors declare a tax revolt? Terrorist bombings and assaults of polling locations leading to suspended elections?

In this scenario, there is no plan. Just increasing chaos and political violence. Political leaders, despite all the evidence to the contrary, keep pinning their hopes on the next election, or the next. Eventually, most likely, it leads to low-grade civil war.

Civil War

Simplifying somewhat, civil wars fall along a spectrum ranging from asymmetric to traditional war. In a traditional war there are identifiable sides, usually organized by geography and competing management. Asymmetric wars may involve multiple, diffuse entities that may or may not be allied in a web of competing interests.

Most observers think that a traditional civil war in the United States is unlikely. My take is that if, say, if the governors and legislatures of Texas and the rest of the South held a press briefing and announced that they wished to unilaterally secede, a traditional civil war would be entirely possible.

The other model, asymmetric warfare, is entirely a matter of degrees. Does the January 6th seizure of Congress count? Bombings? Shootings? Where is the bright line?

For a template for a very likely outcome, consider the Troubles in Ireland[1]. As a worst-case scenario, think Syria[2] -

[1]https://en.wikipedia.org/wiki/The_Troubles
[2]https://en.wikipedia.org/wiki/Syrian_civil_war

in every major American city.

American Dictatorship

If people get scared or intimidated enough, or if a would be dictator is smart enough, it's (sadly) not that hard to imagine an American dictator. First described in the classic *It Can't Happen Here*[3] by Sinclair Lewis in 1935, the roadmap for a takeover of the United States by an authoritarian leader has been clear for a long time.

For more information on this topic, including highly readable analysis of repeated observational data *The Authoritarians*[4] by Bob Altemeyer. It addresses the question "why would anyone follow an authoritarian leader" in detail. In particular I recommend the audiobook version[5] for the highly engaging and humorous delivery of such a fundamentally depressing topic.

Climate Collapse

Eventually, enough political malaise could bring about an end in a chaotic collapse not due to political violence, but by simply being overwhelmed by the impacts of climate change. For example, we have already seen the incidence of hurricanes dramatically increase - what happens if Hurricane Katrina level events become a monthly experience for much

[3]https://amzn.to/3nS2Jx9
[4]https://theauthoritarians.org/
[5]https://amzn.to/3lszmzy

of the year? At some point, the federal government would be forced to either confront trillions of dollars of expense or to simply tell states to begin to manage these issues themselves. It's easy to see these evolving into multi-state compacts, much as happened in the early days of the COVID pandemic.

For many, the last five years (or more) have been a near constant stream of stress, pain and heartache. If this tiny summary isn't enough, check out the essay *Worst Case Scenarios*[6] for more information.

How do we get out of this mess?

---

[6]https://axmoss.com/essays

4. Possible Solutions

There are a few commonly proposed solutions to the broad problem of reform. These include passing legislation, amending the Constitution, breaking into individual states, new entities based on counties, and the solution proposed by this work - multi-state nations.

Pass Legislation

Meaningful legislative reform requires control of the House, Senate, Presidency, and Supreme Court.

1. Control of the House

The House is significantly distorted by gerrymandering, pushing toward more and more intense partisan leanings. The vast majority of House races are effectively single party races, with only the primary serving as an expression of democracy.

2. Filibuster-proof control of the Senate

The allocation of the Senate massively distorts the weight of an individual vote. If you live in Wyoming, one of your Senators represents 284,150 people. In comparison, a Senator from New York represents 9,710,528 people.[1]

---

[1]http://www.thegreenpapers.com/Census10/FedRep.phtml

Apart from budget reconciliation, only 41 Senators can block any legislation via the filibuster. Budget reconciliation is explicitly *not* for resolving the life-and-death issues raised earlier.

3. Control of the Executive

The Electoral College distorts the presidency, with several recent elections no longer reflecting the popular vote. "One Wyoming voter has roughly the same vote power as four New York voters."[2] In addition, the president can veto any bill, forcing a two-thirds vote to confirm in both the House and the Senate.

As if that wasn't enough, the executive increasingly ignores Congress by simply declining to prosecute laws (e.g., marijuana legislation), choosing to insufficiently fund or prioritize an office (e.g. declining to properly fund IRS enforcement), or by pursuing regulatory capture strategies (e.g. appointing oil executives to Department of the Interior offices intended to overseeing the fossil fuel industry).

4. Control of the Supreme Court

The Court, through a series of norm violations, is now wildly out-of-sync with the general population with no viable mechanism for repair or reformation. Both impeachment of a Supreme Court justice and court reform would require legislation, described above.

---

[2]http://www.slate.com/articles/news_and_politics/map_of_the_week/2012/11/ presidential_election_a_map_showing_the_vote_power_of_all_50_states.html

Unfortunately, without changing the Constitution, it is *extraordinarily* unlikely that significant reform can be achieved through legislation.

Fix The Constitution

Fixing the Constitution in the way most people mean - passing amendments to fix particular issues, such as gun control - is in practice obviously much more difficult than passing legislation. To complete the final step (ratification) three-fourths of the states must pass the amendment.

The Constitutional amendment process will be discussed extensively later.

Break into Individual States

Only a few states, such as California and Texas, would be viable as fully independent nations. If the United States split into individual states, the majority of the states would have to associate into multi-state nations again for survival.

Break into Counties

Most people don't really know or understand the complex interactions between the federal, state, county and city governments. From a legal and practical standpoint, breaking up the country into counties (and then potential new nation-states) would be an endless nightmare of complexity.

Break into Multi-State Nations

In this model, the country is reconstituted into six new
nations, organized along commonly recognizable geographic,
cultural, and economic lines. Those existing lines are the
existing states. The question then turns to the precise configu-
ration of which states form into which new nations.

This is the scenario which forms the basis for the rest of
this book.

5. Guidelines for the New Nations of America

When considering a proposal on this scale and scope, it's important to clarify the guiding principles for the division. If you can follow the principles, the division should follow naturally.

With that in mind, here are the guiding principles used to generate the six new nations:

1. Make the initial transition as painless as possible for citizens
2. Use existing state boundaries
3. Use commonly recognized cultural and economic boundaries
4. Target sizes that map to viable autonomous entities
5. Balanced political and economic power

Painless As Possible

For a great many people, they get up, go to school or work, come home, have dinner, and have a nice weekend. They don't know and prefer not to care about the complex legal and economic tapestry that acts as the substrate for their lives.

The day after the split, their money still works. Their contracts and property are still valid. The kids go to the same school. Their city and county and state are all the same.

As a related point, the proposal must be understandable by ordinary people. An overly complex, technocratic solution is unlikely to gain popular support.

Existing State Boundaries

The complexity of the interactions between city, county, state and federal government is staggering. Reconfiguration on other models (for example, by county or drawing up new lines) is simply impractical.

Commonly Recognized Boundaries

Obviously, existing states have well known existing boundaries. You know what state you live in.

So, when it comes to putting the states together in sensible cultural boundaries, I used the book *American Nations: A History of the Eleven Rival Regional Cultures of North America*[1] by Colin Woodard as a primary guide.

---

[1]https://amzn.to/39deneA

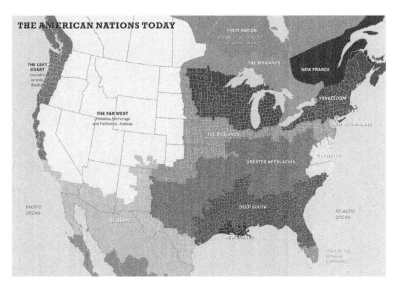

American Nations described by Colin Woodard

You will note that Woodard's maps use county borders, not state. It is not a goal to achieve perfection - perfect alignment along county lines would run directly in counter to the previously stated goals.

If you are wondering how these divisions deal with the rural/urban split, check out the essay *Rural/Urban Divide*[2]. To be clear - the goal is not to create nations that only have urban or rural populations, but rather to create clear, unambiguous and reasonable governance structures. There is no such thing as a large nation that does not have both a rural and urban population mix.

Many other mapmakers develop similar geographic models. For example, the US Census Bureau[3] uses a surprisingly

[2]https://axmoss.com/essays/
[3]https://www.census.gov/geographies/reference-maps/2010/geo/2010-census-regions-and-divisions-of-the-united-states.html

similar division:

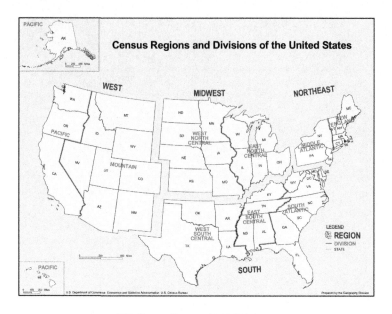

US Census Bureau 2010 Divisions

Many other Federal departments use analogous maps[4]. It only takes a moment to realize why - any large bureaucracy needs to break a large population into components to manage them effectively. At some point any official (public or private) winds up drawing similar maps for similar reasons.

Viable Autonomous Entities

California and Texas could easily survive as independent nations. Rhode Island and Delaware could not. Most other

[4]https://en.wikipedia.org/wiki/List_of_regions_of_the_United_States#Interstate_regions

states would be in a similar position to a smaller or larger degree.

Balanced Power

To be viable, all existing states must be part of a viable demographic and economic whole, on a roughly equal footing. The different nations will have very different profiles, but they must all be treated as equals insofar as possible.

With those principles in place, let's look at a proposed set of new nations.

6. Proposed New Nations

Without further ado, here is a proposal for the six new nations of America:

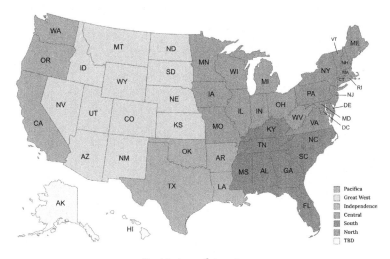

Six Nations of America

The six new nations are as follows, listed west to east. As each new nation would inherit the existing Constitutional structure, they would each start with a much smaller Senate and House. As you review the data, think about how much more effective such smaller legislative bodies would be at governance.

Considerations below include comparative population[1]

---

[1]https://en.wikipedia.org/wiki/List_of_countries_and_dependencies_by_population

figures, comparative GDP[2] figures (including rough GPD comparisons with other nations[3]), maps, and the different cultures as described by *American Nations*[4].

Pacifica

The name celebrates the Pacific Ocean and reflects the gaze to the west.

---

[2]https://en.wikipedia.org/wiki/List_of_states_and_territories_of_the_United_States_by_GDP
[3]https://statisticstimes.com/economy/countries-by-gdp.php
[4]https://en.wikipedia.org/wiki/American_Nations

Pacifica

- Approximate Population: 51.5 million – *roughly the same as Italy or South Korea*
- Approximate GDP: Apx $4.25 trillion – *one of the top five largest economies, somewhere between Japan and Germany*

• Congress: Senate, 6 members; House of Representatives: 68 members

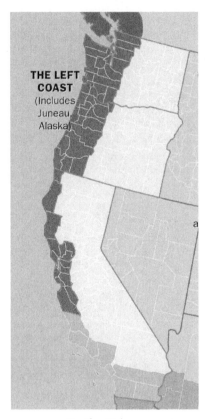

Pacifica Cultures

The dominant cultures[5] of Pacifica are the Left Coast, the Far West and El Norte.

For more information, see the essay *Pacifica*[6].

---

[5]https://en.wikipedia.org/wiki/American_Nations
[6]https://axmoss.com/essays/

Great West

The vast Great West enjoys the most territory and the lowest population of any of the nations.

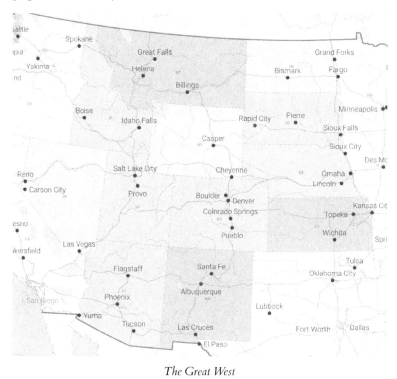

The Great West

- Approximate Population: 29 million - *a bit larger than Australia's 26 million*
- Approximate GDP: Apx $2 trillion - *one of the top ten largest world economies, roughly equal to Italy and larger than Canada*
- Congress: Senate, 22 members; House of Representatives: 37 members

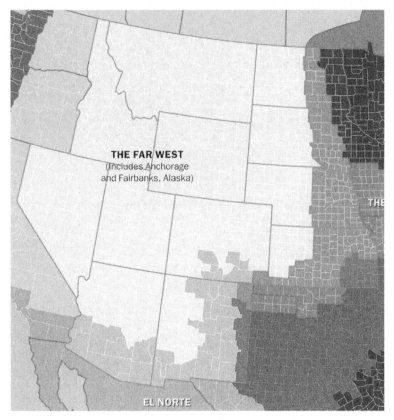

Great West Cultures

The dominant culture[7] of the Great West as described in *American Nations* is the Far West. The eastern portion has a strong Midlands section, and the south El Norte.

The transition to a nation would have an unusually significant impact on the Great West - the vast bulk of the territory is owned by the Federal government[8]. Federal land ownership is significant in Pacifica as well, but not to

---

[7]https://en.wikipedia.org/wiki/American_Nations
[8]https://en.wikipedia.org/wiki/Federal_lands

the extent. Moving land management from Washington D.C. to The Great West would have a huge impact on the governance of this land.

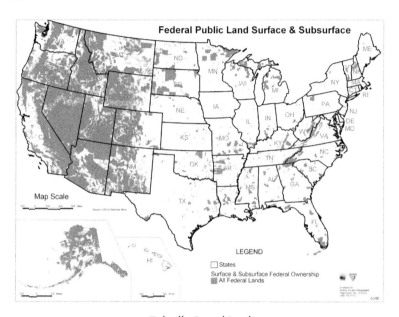

Federally Owned Land

For more information, see the essay *The Great West*[9].

Independence

These fiercely independent territories have a long and complex history of independence.

9https://axmoss.com/essays/

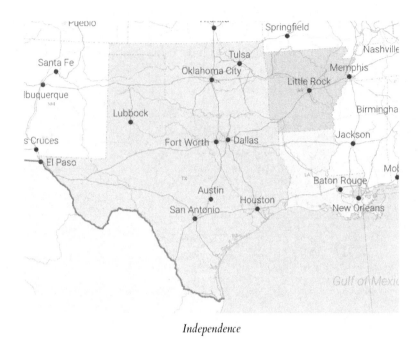

Independence

- Approximate Population: 40.3 million – *a bit larger than Canada's 38 million*
- Approximate GDP: Apx $2.6 trillion – *one of the top ten largest world economies, roughly equal to France*
- Congress: Senate: 8 members; House of Representatives: 51 members

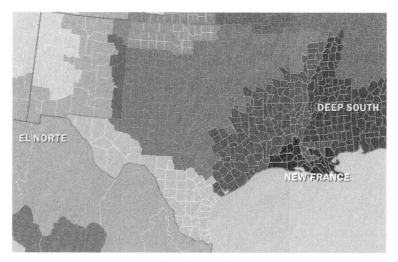

Independence Cultures

The dominant cultures[10] of Independence are a strip of Midlands to the north, a large portion of Greater Appalachia, the Deep South in the east, El Norte in the South, and a complex section of New France.

For more information, see the essay *Independence*[11].

Central

A mighty economic engine, with some of the largest cities in North America.

[10]https://en.wikipedia.org/wiki/American_Nations
[11]https://axmoss.com/essays/

Central

- Approximate Population: 65.6 million - *roughly the same as the United Kingdom*
- Approximate GDP: Apx $4.2 trillion - *one of the top five largest economies, somewhere between Japan and Germany*
- Congress: Senate: 20 members; House of Representatives: 91 members

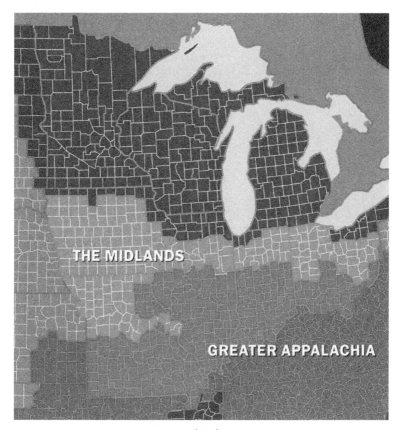

Central Cultures

The dominant cultures[12] of Central are Yankeedom, The Midlands, and Greater Appalachia.

For more information, see the essay *Central*[13].

[12]https://en.wikipedia.org/wiki/American_Nations
[13]https://axmoss.com/essays/

South

The South has (in)famously long sought to break away from the Union.

The South

- Approximate Population: 66.5 million - *roughly the same as the United Kingdom*
- Approximate GDP: Apx $3.8 trillion - *one of the top five largest economies, roughly the same as Germany*

- Congress: Senate: 16 members; House of Representatives: 87 members

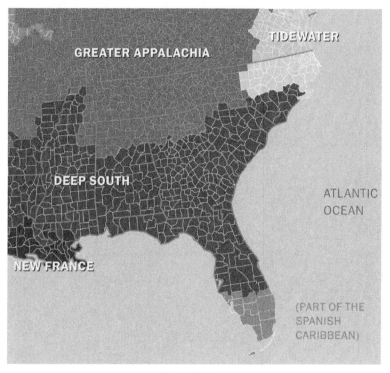

South Cultures

The dominant culture[14] of the South is, of course, the Deep South. A large portion is part of Greater Appalachia. A portion of Tidewater lies in the north-east. The southern end of Florida is Spanish Caribbean. As the economic engine, Florida would play a powerful role in the future of the South.

For more information, see the essay *The South*[15].

[14]https://en.wikipedia.org/wiki/American_Nations
[15]https://axmoss.com/essays/

North

The North has effectively ruled the country, and by proxy, the world since World War 2.

The North

- Approximate Population: 72.9 million - *a bit larger than France's 67 million*
- Approximate GDP: Apx $5.9 trillion - *the second largest economy in the world after China*
- Congress: Senate: 24 members; House of Representatives: 98 members

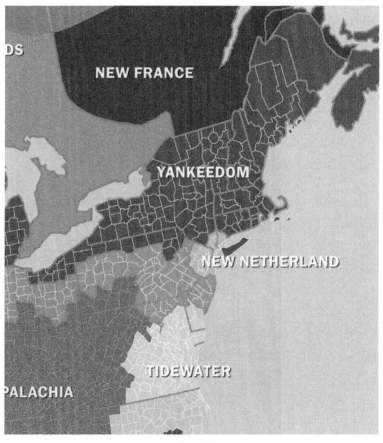

North Cultures

The North is dominated by Yankeedom, New Netherland, a strip of the Midlands, a small bit of Greater Appalachia, and Tidewater.

For more information, see the essay *The North*[16].

The Rest

What about Hawaii and Alaska? And the many territories and holdings possessed by the United States?

A possible outcome might be:

- Hawaii joins Pacifica. Both share a similar contemporary political outlook as well as geographic interests.
- Alaska joins The Great West. Common issues around land management and cultural similarities make for a coherent fusion.

Overseas territories to the west of the Panama Canal and east of South Africa would most likely transfer to Pacifica. Similarly, territories to the east of the Panama Canal and west of South Africa would transfer to the North.

That said, the independence movement in Hawaii and the status of Puerto Rico would both suggest a more complex conversation. Perhaps Hawaii, Alaska, and Puerto Rico would prefer to transition to new nations, allied under the American Union (as described later in this work) instead?

Existing Native American obligations and treaties[17] would transfer from the existing federal government to the enclosing

---

[16]https://axmoss.com/essays/
[17]https://en.wikipedia.org/wiki/Native_Americans_in_the_United_States

new nation. Native American civil rights[18] are a complex topic.

Given all of these complexities, these two states and the various holdings have been omitted from the figures and maps for the new nations. For more information, see the essay *The Rest*[19].

Now that we have a sense of the new nations, let's consider how to make this happen – and then we'll look at the new American Union.

---

[18]https://en.wikipedia.org/wiki/Native_American_civil_rights
[19]https://axmoss.com/essays/

7. How To Make It Happen

Passing a Constitutional amendment is a superficially simple process.[1]

The amendment first must be **proposed** by either:

- a two-third majority vote in both the House of Representatives and the Senate, or
- by a constitutional convention called for by two-thirds (34 of 50) of the State legislatures.

None of the 27 amendments to the Constitution have been proposed by constitutional convention.

A proposed amendment becomes part of the Constitution as soon as it is **ratified** by three-fourths of the States (38 of 50 States).[2]

The process is almost totally **driven by states, not population**. As we know from earlier discussions, this means the entire amendment process is heavily biased toward rural populations.

To put these ratification numbers in perspective, 30 states voted for Trump in 2016 (25 in 2020). Only four more states

---

[1]The material in this chapter summarizing the Constitutional amendment process is based primarily on a highly abbreviated summary of the description provided by the National Archives website.

[2]Most people mean "ratify" when they say "pass" regarding amendments. Unfortunately, this can get a bit confusing. For example, a state might "pass" a referendum requesting an amendment, the state legislature might then "pass" the amendment to then be proposed, and then it might be "passed" again when finally ratified.

would be needed to begin the process, and only eight more to ratify the amendment.

Among other things, moving forward requires:

- A political entity to advocate for and organize the process (including presenting a reasonably solid draft amendment)
- Political pressure/cover for state legislatures and/or
- Political pressure/cover for federal legislators

That's it.

The Last Amendment

The Twenty-seventh Amendment (Amendment XXVII) to the United States Constitution prohibits any law that increases or decreases the salary of members of Congress from taking effect until after the next election of House of Representatives has occurred. It is the most recently adopted amendment but was one of the first proposed. [...]

The proposed congressional pay amendment was largely forgotten until 1982, when Gregory Watson, a 19-year-old sophomore at the University of Texas at Austin, wrote a paper for a government class in which he claimed that the amendment could still be ratified. An unconvinced teaching assistant graded the paper poorly, motivating Watson to launch a nationwide campaign to complete its ratification. The amendment eventually became part of the United States Constitution, effective May 5, 1992, completing a record-setting ratification period of 202 years, 7 months, and 10 days, beating the previous record set by the Twenty-second Amendment of 3 years and 343 days.

• Wikipedia*a*

*a*https://en.wikipedia.org/wiki/Twenty-seventh_Amendment_to_the_ United_States_Constitution

Political Pressure

The most straightforward, direct and clear way to state a political preference is to begin with the referendum and initiative systems. The language for the referendums/initiatives could be comparatively simple. "We, the people, request the legislature begin the process of amending the Constitution to begin splitting the United States into six new nations" is probably too simple, but a few carefully constructed paragraphs would likely suffice.

If the referendums and initiatives begin to pass and popular opinion shows the idea to be popular *with their base* things could go relatively quickly.

This could easily become a very significant fundraising opportunity for many politicians. It's the final step in the general anti-government rhetoric for the right and the fear on the left of Republican controlled federal

> government.

At some point, this transitions from a high level conversation ("how to pass the Amendment") to the much more complex details of *actually* passing the amendment. This quickly turns into a relatively tactical discussion of topics such as fundraising, setting up a political action committee, etc. For more details on this topic see the essay *Organizing and Passing The Amendment*[3].

For the purposes of these briefs, let's assume that passing an amendment is plausible and reasonable. What would the amendment actually *do*?

Draft Points

Here's an example of the draft language:

- Upon ratification, the following states will form new Nations. Each new Nation will operate under a copy of the existing Constitution, including both existing law and legal precedent.
- The Congress of each new Nation will initially be composed of the House and Senate membership of the prior Congress.
- The President of each new Nation will take office following a new election.

---

[3]https://axmoss.com/essays/

- The Congress of each new Nation will confirm a new Supreme Court.
- Federal lands in each new Nation, including military bases, will be transferred to the new government of the containing Nation.
- The Federal Reserve and existing Dollar will continue, with new Federal Reserve Governors appointed by the Congress of each new Nation according to the existing schedule, i.e. one every two years. For a period of no less than ten years from ratification, each new Nation agrees to maintain the United States Dollar as the official currency.
- For a period of no less than ten years from ratification, each new Nation agrees to maintain existing open borders between Nations. These borders would allow for the same open transport as exists today between States, with existing port and immigration authority maintained by the new Nations.
- The existing Federal Debt will be assumed by each Nation in proportion to population.
- Nuclear weapons and transferable military assets will be assumed by each new Nation in proportion to GDP.
- Federal headcount will initially be allocated between the nations on a GDP basis.
- All nations will receive copies of all information resources of the existing federal government, including research and intelligence information.
- Each new Nation will initially be bound by existing foreign relations and trade agreements. Each Nation will

have right to negotiate new foreign relations and trade
agreements going forward.

- Each Nation may amend their Constitution independently.
- Each new Nation may enter into trade and other
  agreements with each other.
- All current United States Citizens and Corporations
  must declare within a period of one year their new
  nation for purposes of Citizenship. If a Citizen or Corporation does not explicitly declare, their Citizenship will
  be determined by their primary residence or location of
  their primary headquarters.
- The residents of US territories would hold referendums
  on which new Nation they wish to join or to choose
  independence.

This is barely over three hundred words, and it captures
the spirit and text reasonably well. For the vast majority of
ordinary citizens of the United States, the day after ratification
little would change on a practical level. All of their existing
contracts and property rights would continue. They would
continue to use the dollar, presumably still relying heavily on
credit cards for day-to-day transactions. The kids would still
go to school. The Social Security checks would still show up.
Taxes would still be collected and paid.

8. The Split

The process (conceptually) is straight-forward.

1. A new Constitutional amendment is passed. The current federal government is split into six new nations.
2. Each new nation starts off with an *exact copy* (or fork[1]) of the existing Constitution.
3. The existing federal government, including all income, assets, and debts, are then allocated to these new nations.
4. The Federal Reserve (and the dollar) will continue to exist, essentially unchanged.[2] This and the prior point are discussed in the brief *Allocating The Federal Government*.
5. For most people, very little changes at first. Contracts, property, money, jobs, regulations, legal precedent - on day one it's a non-event.
6. All existing treaties remain in effect for all parties. For example, all six nations are still NATO members and are therefore mutually obligated to defend each other. All six member are still parties to trade agreements such as the

---

[1] A software development term. The idea of a fork is that at a specific point in time two sets of documents diverge to serve different needs.

[2] Currently the Board of Governors for the Federal Reserve System consists of seven members. Under this proposal, six of the seven would come from the new nations. The seventh would be the Chairman, selected by the other members. When a Chairman is selected, the term would be for four years and then that Chairman would step down from the FDR.

new NAFTA and international memberships such as the
United Nations.

7. For a ten year "cooling off" period, most inter-nation
   relationships stay the same. In particular, freedom of
   movement and interstate trade remain open.
8. A new entity called the American Union (AU), will be
   created to manage various inter-nation issues. This is
   discussed in the brief *American Union*.
9. Subject to the rules and guidelines above, each new
   nation could then begin to amend their Constitution,
   develop new legal precedent, and otherwise begin self-
   governance.

What About Corporations?

In the short term, most corporations wouldn't be affected all
that much. They would have to declare their new Nation,
which would be used for both legal charter and taxation. For
various reasons, certain states today (in particular, Delaware)
are unusually popular for corporate formation. If a corporation based in California wished to continue to be registered in
Delaware, that would presumably lead to taxation as a foreign
corporation. It's easy to imagine that enterprising nations
would offer one-time tax breaks in exchange for repatriation
of funds and transfer of corporate formation. The corporations
would be fine.

Things would change over time. The new nations would
evolve different rules for everything from worker rights to
environmental restrictions. Taxation, of course, would wildly

diverge as well. The wheels of democracy would keep on turning.

Refugees and Political Minorities

A common conversation topic that came up during the drafting of this material is the notion of political refugees.

For example, let's say you are a big fan of Trump and generally agree with his positions. Under this model, if you are living in rural California, are you worse off than before? Similarly, what about minorities living in the South?

This is already a big problem for many, and as noted at the beginning of this work, not all problems can or will be solved by splitting into six new nations. Reproductive rights are a matter of concern for in the South today, not as an abstract concept. In other words, this proposal cannot fix all of our cultural problems, but it can take the pressure off and (as described above) move us away from civil war.

It is precisely these concerns about minority rights across the board that drives the concept of a ten year cooling off period. That's enough time for minority residents to make a decision about their best options in an orderly fashion. It's also enough time for the new nations to decide how govern themselves and interact with each other.

For example, the new nations of Independence and The South might decide that their best strategy is to create as open an economic environment as possible, while also increasing the coupling of religion and government. Pacifica might decide that increased taxes and a rich social network is a better strategy, perhaps modeling itself more explicitly after

Scandinavian nations. In that scenario, each of those nations may decide to offer immigration packages specifically targeted at the people they want to encourage to move to their nation. Those immigration packages might go so far as to explicitly offer political refugee status to groups they wish to support.

This all gets very, very complicated very quickly. In practice, I find that it acts as a very interesting form of Rorschach test[3] for how people regard the different regions. In other words, by simply listening to how you describe another region and how you imagine they will treat political minorities can be very revealing.

A few questions as a thought experiment - would you support a program that would give someone a one time relocation package to leave their current state and move to your state? Would you support more aggressive federal involvement to enforce federal laws (such as Eisenhower in Little Rock[4])? Does your opinion on this matter change depending on which president is enforcing which order?

These are tricky topics, and they really drive to the original premise of this proposal. As a nation, we don't want the same outcomes, and it's increasingly difficult to sort this out with our existing federal system.

Ten Year Cooling Off Period

For a period of ten years after passage, the six Nations would agree to maintain several key portions of the existing union. These include:

[3]https://en.wikipedia.org/wiki/Rorschach_test
[4]https://en.wikipedia.org/wiki/Little_Rock_Nine

- Freedom of movement
- Respect for current inter-state relations, such as existing trade and regulatory commitments
- Proceed with the orderly transfer of federal assets to the new nations - everything from staff to land to physical assets
- Commitment to good faith resolution of disputes and cooperation

During this period, the existing Federal government would continue to function, but with the primary goal being the orderly transition of staff and resources.

Of all of these, the single most important is likely to be freedom of movement. It's entirely possible that many people may find themselves drawn to one new nation or another once the nations begin diverging. For example, one nation may pass an amendment declaring itself to be an explicitly Christian nation, banning abortion. Another might choose to raise taxes, legalize drugs, and establish a universal basic income for all citizens. It's pretty easy to imagine individuals deciding that their personal values are much more aligned with one nation or another. Ten years is enough time for them to make that decision, find a new job, sell the house, or otherwise take action as they see fit.

Ten years is also enough time for things to sink in and for the heat and passions around breaking apart to really sink in. As various figures confront the reality of the transition, they will also have ample time to consider the nature of any future American Union.

A few sections refer to maintaining currency and open borders for a period of ten years. The intent is to maintain continuity, while also opening the door for future agreements and negotiations. Some Nations may wish to enforce strong border security, enacting walls and strict controls, whereas others may not wish to make such strategic decisions. Similarly, adherence to the United States Dollar, the world's reserve currency, is of tremendous value. I would expect that the economic benefits of a single currency would outweigh any advantages to be found by breaking away, but that would be a decision for the future politicians and citizens. At least one new Nation may wish to experiment with a Brexit-style split after the initial decade of integration. It's likely that the outcome of the actual Brexit will heavily influence that perspective.

Before considering any details about any future American Union, let's examine the Federal government in more detail.

9. Allocating the Federal Government

The scale and scope of the United States federal government can seem overwhelming at first. We usually get an orientation in the basic operating agreements in school (the Constitution, the three branches of government, etc.) but the day-to-day operation is less well understood.

As a large organization, the federal government can first be understood as an entity that takes in revenue, then spends that revenue to accomplish goals. It might spend the money in the form of checks, perhaps as salary for staff or as payments to individuals or corporations. The staff and resource purchase are typically broken down into civilian and military expenditures.

With that in mind, let's start reviewing what the federal government does just like any other organization - revenue, expenditures, organization and assets (in particular, land).

Here is the summary of the federal government revenue based on Congressional Budget Office (CBO) data for 2020:[1]

---

[1] All of summary infographics in this brief are taken from the CBO summary for 2020. https://www.cbo.gov/system/files/2021-04/57170-budget-infographic.pdf. From the summary: *All data are for federal fiscal years, which run from October 1 to September 30. Numbers may not add up to totals because of rounding.*

Revenue

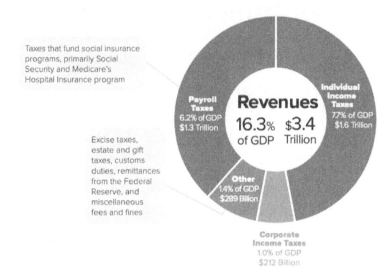

CBO - Federal Government Revenue 2020

The vast majority of revenue (apx. $2.9 trillion) is either direct individual income taxes or payroll taxes (paid by workers, managed by via payroll deductions). Corporate income taxes and "other" together account for only apx. $501 billion.

Revenues account for 16.3% of GDP – three out of every twenty dollars spent each year are collected by the federal government.

Expenditures

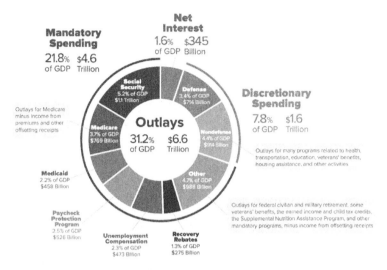

Mandatory Spending
21.8% $4.6
of GDP Trillion

Net Interest
1.6% $345
of GDP Billion

Discretionary Spending
7.8% $1.6
of GDP Trillion

Outlays for many programs related to health, transportation, education, veterans' benefits, housing assistance, and other activities

Social Security
5.2% of GDP
$1.1 Trillion

Defense
3.4% of GDP
$714 Billion

Medicare
3.7% of GDP
$769 Billion

Outlays for Medicare minus income from premiums and other offsetting receipts

Outlays
31.2% $6.6
of GDP Trillion

Nondefense
4.4% of GDP
$914 Billion

Medicaid
2.2% of GDP
$458 Billion

Other
4.7% of GDP
$988 Billion

Paycheck Protection Program
2.5% of GDP
$526 Billion

Outlays for federal civilian and military retirement, some veterans' benefits, the earned income and child tax credits, the Supplemental Nutrition Assistance Program, and other mandatory programs, minus income from offsetting receipts

Unemployment Compensation
2.3% of GDP
$473 Billion

Recovery Rebates
1.3% of GDP
$275 Billion

CBO - Federal Government Revenue 2020

Expenditures account for 31.2% of GDP, or just a little under one in three dollars spent each year.

The bulk of the Federal expenditures basically amount to sending out checks. These expenditures include (roughly in order of size) Social Security, Medicare, Medicaid, Paycheck Protection Program[2], Unemployment, and Recovery Rebates[3].

Defense accounts for $714 billion, or roughly 3.4% of GDP.

All other Federal government expenditures represent roughly a quarter of the budget. Many of these programs

---

[2]A temporary SBA program to assist businesses during COVID.
[3]A temporary program to send individual cash payments during COVID.

also mainly involve sending checks - for example, retirement
plans, earned income and child tax credits.

It is notable some of the most consequential activities
of the federal government are effectively too small to even
register on the multi-trillion dollar scale of the federal budget.
These include (but are not limited to):

- Regulatory functions (for example, the FDA, EPA,
  OSHA, SEC, and others[4])
- The court system, including the Supreme Court
- NASA and basic science investments
- Backstop guarantor for student loans

An analysis by David Coleman[5] walks through the
government staff levels, including breakdowns by branch of
government and civilian/military levels. While the process
of breaking up the staff of the federal government may seem
overwhelming, civilian employment by the federal government is roughly equivalent to the staff level of Walmart, and
the employee count for the military is roughly similar to that
of Amazon.[6] Considering that Amazon was only founded in
1995[7], it seems entirely possible to reconfigure an existing
bureaucracy given the application of sufficient time and
energy.

---

[4]Wildly over-simplified: The FDA makes sure our food and drugs are safe. The EPA
regulates pollution. OSHA regulates worker safety. The SEC regulates the stock market.
While you may disagree with certain aspects of these (and many other) regulatory
programs, most would regard them as key foundations of modern American society.

[5]https://historyinpieces.com/research/federal-personnel-numbers-1962

[6]https://companiesmarketcap.com/largest-companies-by-number-of-employees/

[7]https://en.wikipedia.org/wiki/History_of_Amazon

Debt

You may have noticed that the revenue for 2020 was $3.4 trillion (16.3% of GDP) and the expenditures were $6.6 trillion (31.2% of GDP). This gap is closed by issuing debt. Federal debt is held by a mix[8] of domestic ($_{60}$%) and foreign entities (40%).

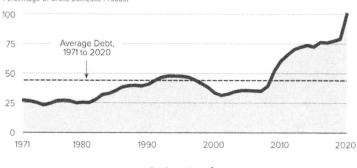

Federal Debt Held by the Public, 1971 to 2020
Percentage of Gross Domestic Product

CBO: US Debt

The debt as a ratio of GDP high on a historic basis for the United States. It is, however, relatively typical for a large nation[9] – it's essentially identical to France (99%), Belgium (99%), and Spain (99%). It's nowhere near the level of Japan (237%), Greece (174%), or Italy (133%). Compared to Germany (57%) it's quite high.

Oversimplifying, the Federal debt went from an average level of roughly just under 50% of GDP until the recession of 2008. The various stimulus programs and tax cuts after the

---

[8]https://usafacts.org/data/topics/government-finances/debt/obligations-and-national-debt/of-federal-debt-held-by-public-that-is-foreign-owned/
[9]https://worldpopulationreview.com/countries/countries-by-national-debt

2008 recession caused the debt to spike to roughly 75%. The response to COVID in turn caused it to rise to roughly 100%.

The Dollar & The Federal Reserve

The current Federal Reserve is managed by a board of seven, with one of the members serving as the Chairman[10]. After the split, the seats would be filled by rotation between the six new nations - one every two years.

Otherwise, the Federal Reserve would continue to operate as it does today. The real challenge for the Federal Reserve - as today - is working with the various legislatures on managing the debt load and spending by each of the six new nations. The dollar, however, would remain managed independently.

The Easy Stuff

From the perspective of breaking up the United States federal government into six nations, the vast majority of the income, expenditures and debt are (conceptually) pretty straight-forward.

Instead of the revenue going to a single IRS office, it goes to one of six. The interest payments and various direct money government programs continue as today. If you live in, say, California, you will send in your taxes to the Pacifica IRS, and you would get your Social Security check from the Pacifica Social Security Administration.

---

[10]https://www.federalreserve.gov/aboutthefed/bios/board/default.htm

The current federal debt would be allocated by GDP percentages.

Eventually, as the different nations evolved and passed new legislation, things would change. At least to start, money in, money out as usual.

Regulatory & Science

Initially all of the existing regulatory bodies would be replicated for each of the six nations. Each nation would have a FDA[11], a SEC[12], an OSHA[13], etc. Some of these would like be much busier than others (for example, the SEC in the North would likely be considerably larger than the SEC in the Great West).

Most bureaucracies already have geographic splits – as shown in earlier maps, the federal government already uses geographic regions to split things up just as a natural part of a management hierarchy.

Federal Land

The majority of land owned by the federal government[14] is located in Alaska and western states.

---

[11]https://www.fda.gov/
[12]https://en.wikipedia.org/wiki/U.S._Securities_and_Exchange_Commission
[13]https://www.osha.gov/
[14]https://en.wikipedia.org/wiki/Federal_lands

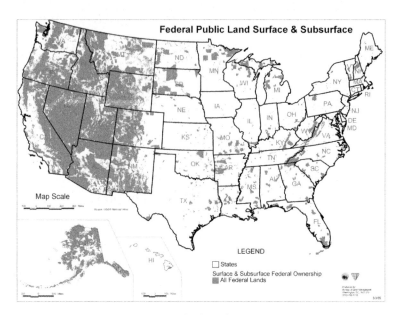

Federal Lands

Federal land would pass to the various new nations based on state boundaries as well. For the Great West and Pacifica, it would be transformative.

Military

The United States military is inarguably one of the most powerful organizations in the world. For the purposes of this brief, we will consider this only from an extremely high level and address much of the complexity in the essay *Military Power Reimagined*[15].

The United States currently spends approximately $778

---

[15]https://axmoss.com/essays/

billion annually. The next closest[16] is China, which spends $252 billion, India at $73 billion, and Russia at $62 billion. Even if the United States split current spending *six ways* between the various new six nations ($130 billion each), *all six nations* would have larger military budgets than every other nation in the world except for China.

Assuming an equal budget split, any two of the new nations (for example, Pacifica and the North), combined with the European Union[17] (~$220 billion) would have nearly double the military budget of China.

Military Staff

As of this writing, the US Armed Forces number roughly 1.35 million.[18] Split evenly, that represents roughly 225,000 active duty personnel for each of the six nations, although in practice this is likely to vary along population and economic figures. For comparison, the world-wide staff for Starbucks[19] in 2020 was 349,000 - a lot of people, to be sure, but not unmanageable.

Military Bases

The United States military possesses a massive number of overseas bases. Domestic bases would go to the enclosing

---

[16]https://en.wikipedia.org/wiki/List_of_countries_by_military_expenditures

[17]https://www.macrotrends.net/countries/EUU/european-union/military-spending-defense-budget

[18]This and other high level US Armed Forces figures in this section taken from https://en.wikipedia.org/wiki/United_States_Armed_Forces.

[19]https://www.macrotrends.net/stocks/charts/SBUX/starbucks/number-of-employees

nation.

For a variety of logistical and historic reasons, overseas bases closest to the Atlantic would likely be financed and managed by the North, and the Pacific bases managed by Pacifica. The 25th latitude would be a reasonable division line. The most significant exception would likely be the South and Independence, managing various assets in the Caribbean, Central and South America.

Specifically, the North would take over Africa, Central, and European Command. Pacifica would take over the Indo-Pacific Command. Southern Command would likely be split between Independence and the South, perhaps splitting again along the lines of the former Caribbean Command.

Land, Sea, and Air Assets

Military assets are difficult to measure and compare. For example, the United States military aircraft (just over 13,000) includes just under 2,000 fighter/interceptors. How does that inventory compare to, say, the Russian military? Quality and quantity both make this difficult to compare[20].

Similarly, the US Navy currently has nine active Carrier Strike Groups[21]. These carrier groups are a fundamental core of the ability of the United States to project power overseas.

The allocation of these various assets would likely be one of the most complex negotiations between the various nations. In the end, a combination of logistics, cost, and negotiations

---

[20]https://www.globalfirepower.com/country-military-strength-detail.php?country_id=united-states-of-america

[21]https://en.wikipedia.org/wiki/Carrier_strike_group

between the civilian leadership of the different nations will necessarily drive the allocations.

Nuclear Power

According to public data, the United States currently possesses 6,185 nuclear warheads, with 3,800 currently part of the active U.S. stockpile.

As of July 2021, American nuclear forces on land consist of 400 Minuteman III ICBMs spread among 450 operational launchers. Those in the seas consist of 14 nuclear-capable Ohio-class Trident submarines, nine in the Pacific and five in the Atlantic. Nuclear capabilities in the air are provided by 60 nuclear-capable heavy bombers, 20 B-2 bombers and 40 B-52s.

- Wikipedia, *Nuclear Weapons of the United States*[a]

[a]https://en.wikipedia.org/wiki/Nuclear_weapons_of_the_United_States

---

The 14 Ohio-class submarines[22] each can carry 24 missiles, each of which can carry 8 independently targeted warheads - in other words, *each* of these 14 submarines can carry and launch 192 nuclear warheads. A single nuclear weapon represents a stunning capability to destroy and kill on a mass scale.[23] Even the largest nations would scarcely survive the

---

[22]https://en.wikipedia.org/wiki/Ohio-class_submarine

[23]https://nuclearsecrecy.com/nukemap/ for an interactive tool to explore the mass destruction capabilities of nuclear weapons.

loss of a dozen major cities – arguably a single Ohio-class submarines is capable of triggering World War III and the end of civilization as we know it.

Assuming all six nations divided the nuclear weapons equally, that's still over six hundred warheads *each*. Only Russia would have more nuclear weapons as a single nation-state.

Military Organization

When most think of the United States military, they think of it in terms of the various branches (e.g. Army, Navy, Air Force, etc.).

In addition to these branches, the military uses unified combatant commands. In a sense, the branches act as resource management, and the unified commands as operational deployment. "There are currently 11 unified combatant commands and each are established as the highest echelons of military commands, in order to provide effective command and control of all U.S. military forces, regardless of branch of service, during peace or during war time. Unified combatant commands are organized either on a geographical basis (known as "area of responsibility", AOR) or on a functional basis, i.e. special operations, force projection, transport, and cybersecurity."[24]

---

[24]https://en.wikipedia.org/wiki/Unified_combatant_command

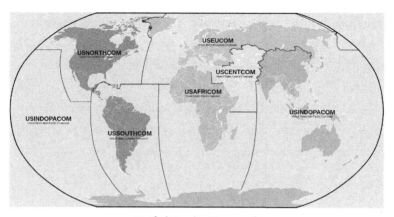

Unified Combat Commands

The Congressional Research Service prepared a report in 2013[25] on the Unified Command Plan for Congress that provides a very readable summary of how the UCC interacts with the rest of the military to implement policy.

For continuity, each of the new nations would likely start by maintaining the current structure blending the army, navy, and other branches with the current UCC system. It's easy to imagine Pacifica taking on primary responsibility for the Pacific deployments (which includes China), and the North handling the European deployment (which includes Russia). The rest could be managed via American Union management (similar to how European nations contribute to NATO and the EU).

Any review of the allocation of federal resources, including the military, quickly reveals geographic allocations along similar lines. Even the US Military amateur endurance sports program[26] uses geographic regions to organize. It's just how

---

[25]https://crsreports.congress.gov/product/pdf/R/R42077/11
[26]https://usmes.org/programs/regions/

large bureaucracies work. While reorganizing bureaucracies certainly takes effort, it's obviously preferable to undertake that endeavor in lieu of the worst case scenarios described earlier.

The discussion of China, Russia and other matters of foreign diplomacy, inextricably tied into military investment, is continued further in the essay *Geo-Political Impacts*[27].

---

[27]https://axmoss.com/essays/

10. American Union

If you have read this far, you likely find the idea of splitting into six nations at least *somewhat* interesting. It might seem a bit peculiar to then pivot to the notion of a new American Union, but it is worth at least considering the benefits of reimagining the relationship between these new nations.

When the original thirteen colonies broke away from the British Empire, they had very good reasons for uniting. Probably the single most compelling was mutual defense - simply put, the odds that one of the European powers would start meddling or scheming to take over one or more independent colonies was high.

The first take at unity, the Articles of Confederation, were simply too weak to respond effectively to threats. This led directly to the current Constitution, which arguably at the signing still represented a relatively weak union. It took the Civil War to really begin unification, and the combination of the Great Depression, the New Deal, World War II, and the Cold War to completely seal the nation into a coherent whole.

Today, we have many different models for integration. In addition to the current Constitution, the Commonwealth and the European Union both serve as examples of different forms of integration.

For those not familiar with the Commonwealth, it's a legacy of the British Empire.

The Commonwealth is a voluntary association of 54 independent and equal countries. It is home to 2.4 billion people, and includes both advanced economies and developing countries.

Our members work together to promote prosperity, democracy and peace, amplify the voice of small states, and protect the environment.

- https://thecommonwealth.org/

Commonwealth Nations Map

The Commonwealth reflects a complex shared history, but it doesn't reflect a terribly deep integration between member states. Few Americans have even heard of the the Commonwealth, as it pretty much never enters into diplomatic or military discussions. For that matter, it rarely even comes up in discussions of such benign topics as humanitarian aid.

Contrast the Commonwealth with the European Union.

European Union Member States

The European Union[1], with 27 member nations, is a much deeper form of integration. A single currency, freedom of movement, complex trade relationships – the scale and scope of the European Union is remarkable. Perhaps most astonishing, the EU currently has an estimated population of about 447 million – quite a bit larger than the United States.

It's entirely possible that the United States could split into six new nations, and simply by adhering to current treaties and relationships such as the UN, NATO, and NAFTA 2.0 after the transition everyone might just be fine. Eventually,

---

[1]https://en.wikipedia.org/wiki/European_Union

this might mean border administration analogous to the borders between the United States and Canada.

That said, there are some matters which would seem to indicate that an American Union would be desirable. Broadly speaking, these might include matters of economics, military, and diplomatic cooperation. Perhaps even matters such as climate change will be addressed with a different dynamic in place.

At a minimum, the American Union would serve as a legal wrapper for basic integration. It might eventually wind up be more comprehensive in approach than the Commonwealth, and less integrated than the European Union. The ten year cooling off period is key not just for continuity, but also to help everyone get clear about what is (and isn't needed).

For more information on this topic, see the essay *American Union*[2].

---

[2]https://axmoss.com/essays/

11. Next Steps

The most common reaction to the material in this book is "ok, but... could this ever possibly happen?"

Well... maybe?

Any political idea goes through a variety of stages. First, a wild idea - often initially expressed in a fantastical setting, such as science fiction. It might be idea from a wild paper in college, or even an evolution through a think tank.

Perhaps it's a book (like this one). Obviously, the single most important thing you can do is to buy a copy for all of your friends and family. Ahem.

If people are interested enough in the idea it starts to break into media circles. In the 2020s, this may very well involve a natural back-and-forth of articles and videos and tweets. Some may simply present the idea and ask their audience to comment. Others may take a more dramatic stand, pro or con.

At some point, if the idea is sufficiently interesting, it may very well move from relative obscurity to more mainstream discussion[1]. Then, at some point, a combination of activists, politicians and organizers may very well take the idea on, push for initiatives, referendums, and/or legislation. Perhaps a few states at first, then more, and then it's taken up at the federal level.

[1]https://en.wikipedia.org/wiki/Overton_window

Here are some relatively modern issues that either have roughly followed this arc and/or are currently in progress:

- Marijuana legalization
- Drug decriminalization
- LGBTQ+ marriage and rights
- Aerosol CFC bans
- Climate change (specific and general measures)
- Universal basic income

Some of these issues have clear leaders - for example, Andrew Yang is closely associated with universal basic income, which he used as a key issue to propel to the national stage. Others contribute with funding and support without explicitly entering politics. In Washington state, Rick Steves, more popularly known for his European travels and TV show, was a major factor in passing marijuana legalization[2].

It is the life and death nature of these issues that makes them so powerful. The existential nature of the collapse of the United States into civil war or dictatorship is no different.

Individual Action

If you are personally engaged by this idea, the first thing to do is talk to friends and family. You probably already know who would be excited by the idea, and who probably wouldn't be. Generally speaking I have found both Democrats and Republicans to be increasingly interested in the idea over the last few years, much as the polling from YouGov indicated.

---

[2]https://www.ricksteves.com/about-rick/drug-policy-reform

Next, see if there is an organization, non-profit, or political action group in your area that is interested in the idea. If you really want to contribute, send money and/or offer to participate, just like any other political cause.

> Pay careful attention to the groups you contribute to – make sure the leadership and the finances are transparent, and that they clearly explain what, where, and how much of the money goes to the cause you are supporting.

Ask elected officials for their thoughts. Press them on how and when they think they can *realistically* accomplish goals in a reasonable timeline. Pay close attention to how they talk about their approach to legislation, ask them about all of the challenges, and what their alternatives are.

Often, Democrat officials and politicians will talk about going back and voting again, voting more, and trying to reach for the impossible – for example, a filibuster proof majority in the Senate. Reconfiguring the Supreme Court. Ending gerrymandering. Press them on exactly how and when that will happen.

On the other side, many of the more desperate Republicans have been making more and more strident calls for violence. Think long and hard about the utter insanity of calls for political violence. Do you *really* think that violent take overs of government buildings or terrorist attacks are going to bring about the change you want?

Organized Action

If you really want to make this happen, start organizing. Start fundraising. There are a lot of great books on the topic. Some examples:

- *Effective Frontline Fundraising*[3] by Jeff Stauch
- *Developing A Nonprofit Business*[4] by Robin Devereaux-Nelson
- *The Little Book of Gold: Fundraising for Small (and Very Small) Nonprofits*[5] by Erik Hanberg
- *Compelling Conversations for Fundraisers: Talk Your Way to Success with Donors and Funders*[6] by Janet Levine, Laurie A Selik

> One of the most tragic aspects of modern American politics is the continuing practices of grift masquerading as political action groups and non-profits.
>
> Don't be a grifter. It's immoral, takes resources away from the cause you are trying to support, and very well may end with fines and/or imprisonment.

Perhaps you may want to run for office yourself, perhaps in addition to starting a non-profit.

---

[3] https://www.apress.com/us/book/9781430239000
[4] https://amzn.to/2ZzE1s9
[5] https://amzn.to/39NhDxw
[6] https://amzn.to/3ocMTOM

- *Run for Something: A Real-Talk Guide to Fixing the System Yourself*[7] by Amanda Litman
- *How To Run For Congress. A Practical Guide*[8] by Allan Levene
- *Becoming a Candidate*[9] by Jennifer L. Lawless

If you already have a platform – in particular, if you have a popular Twitter account or YouTube channel focused on history, social science, or politics – run a video on the topic and see what happens.

A reasonably realistic, concrete goal for an individual looking to get the ball rolling is to focus on a referendum or initiative on the topic.

How Close Are We?

I would submit that all thirty states that Trump won in 2016[10] would be pretty easy targets for fundraising and then passing a referendum or initiative. Simply put, I doubt that anyone who voted for Trump in 2016 is an advocate for a strong federal system, and moving to more local control is almost certainly going to be more appealing.

Keep in mind that only thirty-four states are needed to begin the amendment process, and thirty-eight to ratify. Simply adding in California, Oregon, Washington and one other state would be sufficient.

---

[7] https://amzn.to/2XQcOk9
[8] https://amzn.to/3igoVhD
[9] https://amzn.to/3CORMBu
[10] https://www.aol.com/article/news/2017/07/05/how-many-states-did-trump-win-state-by-state-look-back-2016-presidential-election/23017643/

Twenty six states have a direct referendum and/or initiative system[11]. All but one state have a model in which the legislature can request a state-wide referendum[12].

Perhaps the most straight-forward way for this scenario to unfold is with a single referendum in California. Imagine a scenario in which the federal government undertakes action that the majority of California views as an existential issues. For example, a conservative Supreme Court that, over the course of a single summer, issues one or more of the following rulings:

- Ending affirmative action
- Ending the EPA
- Ending gun control laws
- Mandating funding religious schools with government funds
- Ending Roe v. Wade

In this scenario, a secession movement grows very quickly in California over the course of a summer, causing the polling in favor of secession to jump from 45% to 55%. Once California passes this referendum, it's impossible not to imagine similar referendums in Texas and throughout the South. In other words, a single referendum in California is likely all that would be needed to begin the process.

Similarly, it's possible to imagine Republican-controlled state legislatures, as a way to protest the actions of a Democrat-controlled Congress and/or President to call for a

---

[11]https://www.ncsl.org/research/elections-and-campaigns/chart-of-the-initiative-states.aspx

[12]https://en.wikipedia.org/wiki/Initiatives_and_referendums_in_the_United_States

referendum on passing a split. Once the first state legislature passes the first referendum, it could snowball quickly. It would be the final, logical step for fundraising for politicians of all stripes – "Never again be in fear of a Trump takeover" on the left, and "Freedom from liberal tyranny" on the right. It's a thin line from fundraising, to taking a vote, to making it happen.

History is full of far stranger things.

12. Frequently Asked Questions

When reviewing the briefs, there are many common questions and reactions.

Q: It'll never happen!

A: This isn't really a question so much as a statement of faith. To this I would merely note that there are a long, long list of things that would never happen... until they do.

A few examples of things that will "never happen":

- "The colonies will never leave the Empire"
- "We would never shed American blood in a civil war over slavery"
- "England will never leave the European Union"
- "The Soviet Union will never fall"
- "We will never legalize marijuana"
- "We will never legalize gay marriage"
- "The United States will never elect a black man to be president"
- "Trump will never be president"
- "We will never see a violent coup attempt on Congress in broad daylight"
- "Politicians that lie overtly about things like election results can't be elected"

History is... complicated. Virtually every science fiction writer considers the possibility that the United States will be dramatically reconfigured. The United States only added Alaska and Hawaii as states in 1959.

Q: What about the South?

A: This is a big one. Virtually every face-to-face conversation about the topic of breaking up the country inevitably turns into a discussion of the South. Common concerns include:

- The fate of people of color, non-Christians, and the LQBTQ+ community
  - Often expressed as concern that without the Federal government to intervene, the South would begin intense suppression of these groups
- Hostilities
  - Potentially including concerns that South, given the opportunity, might launch nuclear weapons(!) at the North
- Economics
  - Often expressed as concerns that the South would be unable to cover the bills without the largess of the coasts
  - Sometimes cited as reason for the South to mount a military invasion

It's... a lot. These conversations often take on the tone of a therapy session in which the pain of the individual comes to the fore quickly. Some of these wounds are straight-forward (the gay kid that fled the South) - and some are more abstract - the liberal that spent a lifetime compromising on life-or-death issues due to the importance of assembling a national coalition.

It is also worth highlighting that many of the issues that are often brought up by liberals as problems of "the South" are often just as significant in their own states. For example, the racial history of the Oakland/Berkeley area in California is complex and the issues are far-reaching today. Far too often liberal states rely on demonizing other states as a way to deflect from addressing local concerns.

A central premise underlying this work is that if liberal politicians on the west coast and conservative politicians in the south both focus more on delivering results for their constituencies the outcome will be better democracy. Few Democrats on the West coast will miss Mitch McConnell, and few Republicans in the South will miss Nancy Pelosi.

All of this (and more) are discussed in detail in the essay The South[1].

Q: Won't things calm down and make all of this unnecessary?

Possibly. But, sadly, there is a very good chance that *this* is a calm period before things get worse. It's impossible to say.

One theory of history is that things tend to revert to some kind of mean. Under this model, as Republicans become more and more overtly undemocratic, voters will in turn react by rejecting extreme candidates.

---

[1]https://axmoss.com/essays

This theory presupposes the existence of a moderating middle. As has been endlessly discussed, all of the evidence points to a United States that is instead increasingly polarizing. The central premise of this work is that the roots of this polarization can be found in the cultural response to an increasing number of life-or-death issues.

Put another way, there is nothing in the data to show the cultures of the United States are coming together anytime soon. Every school shooting, every officer-involved shooting, every time the government steps in to manage a crisis, every national election - it just gets worse.

Even after the January 6th coup attempt, throughout 2021 Trump remained a nominally viable national candidate despite a 10.6% net unfavorable. Biden's approval rating ended 2021 underwater with a 8.7% net unfavorable, and Harris with an even worse net 15.1% unfavorable. As of the end of 2021 polling data[2] put a matchup between Biden and Trump as an effective coin-toss. Trump would most likely defeat Harris in a landslide. It's hard to imagine the United States surviving a second Trump presidency intact - but as of the end of 2021 the American people were still effectively undecided.

While it would be wonderful for all of the fractures in American society to be healed to the point that this work would be unnecessary, there is little if any data to support that position.

Faith manages. But sometimes it needs a little help.

Q: What is a Nation?

---

[2]https://projects.fivethirtyeight.com/polls/

"The Treaty of Westphalia, which ended the Thirty Years' War in 1648, codified this new understanding. The treaty in many ways established the modern international system, one dominated by countries and the principle of sovereignty. The concept of sovereignty had three basic dimensions. First, countries should accept the borders of other countries and not use force in an attempt to change them. Second, countries should not interfere in events inside other countries. Third, governments should have a free hand to do as they please within their own borders.

— *The World: A Brief Introduction* by Richard Haass

This definition (sometimes referred to as a "Westphalian nation-state") highlights the distinction in terms of relations between nations. I sometimes visualize it as how cells in a body divide up responsibilities - an independent nation may have a high or low degree of autonomy, but there is a membrane that clearly defines the "us" and "them" of a nation.

I would extend this definition in a few ways. First, the notion that the members of a nation generally respect the nation itself as a concept. Second, that the government of the nation has successfully established a monopoly on physical violence.

These two points - legitimacy and violence - are so ancient that many fail to see how pervasive and critical they are to the survival of a nation.

By way of illustration, nations fall when the people of the

nation no longer believe in their governance, or when they are not longer able to protect the people of the nation from physical harm. The latter - physical violence - can be external (war) or internal (rebellion).

Dictators draw legitimacy directly from explicit control of physical violence. Democracies tend to start from legitimacy derived from the vote, and then use that to sustain the use of physical violence.

The intersection of lack of legitimacy and an appeal to physical violence as the resolution is essentially the definition of a rebellion.

13. Essays

For reasons of time and space, this book only includes a series of briefs. These briefs are intended to provide a summary of the ideas for a busy reader.

For those more interested in the details, or with specific questions about certain topics, check out the companion title *A More Perfect Union (Essays)*.

Some of the topics covered include:

- *Who Is Running The Show*, an attempt to try to sort out who (if anyone) is really responsible for how we got into this situation.
- *Worst Case Scenarios*, a review of just how bad things might get if action isn't taken.
- *Split Timeline*, a more detailed look at the timeline for the process.
- *American Union*, examining the model for a new American Union in more detail, with additional compare/contrast information with the European Union.
- *National Unity Projects* covers the challenges of trying to develop unity across incompatible cultural world views.
- More information on the tactical details required for building a movement to pass an amendment on this scale.
- Coverage of the geopolitical implications, including analysis of the implications for China, Russia, the European Union, and more.

- *Rural/Urban Divide* explores the inherently fractal nature of the rural/urban divide and the (hopelessness) of trying to build new nations based on this split.

For more information on *A More Perfect Union (Essays)*, visit https://axmoss.com/.

14. Closing Notes

A few notes in closing.

Not Enough Time

Ideally, I would have had a lot more time to write this book and the companion essays. There are many areas that deserve more analysis and data crunching. A short list of the things I could easily have spent a year or more on:

- Interviews with individuals throughout the nation. Everything from opinions and reactions to discussion of mechanics with experts in various fields.
- Interviews with minority groups in each nation for their thoughts.
- Statistical analysis for the material in several chapters, in particular the theories around the limits of imperial cohesion as the population figures grow.
- More comprehensive analysis of the performance of the European Union and the applicability of various aspects of the EU to the American Union.
- An additional essay on the challenges blending competing values of democracy and minority rights

Unfortunately, events are moving quickly. The polls showing an increased interest in breaking up the nation are as of this writing coming out with increasing frequency (a sign that the Overton window is already expanding). Republican politicians are openly discussing secession. Several others are calling for armed resistance, including public support for the January 6th insurrectionists.

In the end, I'm making a bet. That getting this book out as a template for reconfiguring the United States provides an alternative to violence, insurrection and civil war.

If a single person puts down a gun in favor of pursing a legal alternative after reading this book, it's worth putting it out now.

Suggested Reading

The single most influential book on this work is *American Nations: A History of the Eleven Rival Regional Cultures of North America* by Colin Woodard.

Structural Concerns

These books provide a broader context for the events leading up to today.

- *The World: A Brief Introduction* by Richard Haass
- *The Clash of Civilizations and the Remaking of World Order* by Samuel P. Huntington
- *Capital in the Twenty-First Century* by Thomas Piketty
- *The Big Squeeze* by Steven Greenhouse

- *Collapse: How Societies Choose to Fail or Succeed* and *Upheaval: Turning Points for Nations in Crisis* by Jared Diamond
- *Generations* and/or *Fourth Turning* by William Strauss, Neil Howe

On Secession

These books provide a look at some of the earlier, failed approaches to secession and some additional thoughts on the current interest in secession.

- *Break It Up: Secession, Division, and the Secret History of America's Imperfect Union* by Richard Kreitner
- *American Secession: The Looming Threat of a National Breakup* by F.H. Buckley

American Politics

Discussion of the current state of United States politics and the Republican party.

- *American Carnage: On the Front Lines of the Republican Civil War and the Rise of President Trump* by Tim Alberta
- *Insane Clown President: Dispatches from the 2016 Circus* by Matt Taibbi

Historic Context

Recommended reading (and in one case, viewing).

- *1984* by George Orwell

- *Since Yesterday: The 1930s in America* by Frederick Lewis Allen
- *It Can't Happen Here* by Sinclair Lewis
- *Rise and Fall of the Third Reich* and *Berlin Diary: The Journal of a Foreign Correspondent 1934-1941* by William L. Shirer
- *What Every Person Should Know About War* by Chris Hedges
- Chernobyl (Mini-Series), HBO.

    In Europe: Travels Through the Twentieth Century by Geert Mak
- *A Short History of World War II* by James L. Stokesbury

Looking Forward

Two perspectives on the future of America over the next few decades.

- *The Next Hundred Million: America in 2050* by Joel Kotkin
- *One Billion Americans: The Case for Thinking Bigger* by Matthew Yglesias